> Medical Sales Representatives
>
> Sales Managers
>
> _____
>
> *TAKE CARE OF YOUR BUSINESS RELATIONS !*
>
> Essential Talent for Business
>
> _____

Frantz DALLEMAND

Copyright- February 2016

This book is the intellectual property of

Frantz DALLEMAND

All rights reserved

Legal deposit September 2016

Table of contents

Foreword 5

Introduction. Medical Sales Representatives, Regional Managers, who are they ? 12

1. Take care of your relationships ! 25
   - A. A few general points 25
   - B. Why improve quality? 27
   - C. How can we improve quality? 31
   - D. How to deal with Mr/Mrs UNHAPPY ? 35

2. Take care of your communication ! 41
   - A. What communication is 44
   - B. The art and art of negotiation 47
   - C. List of winning words and attitudes 51
   - D. A little theory 54
   - E. Is your mission well understood by everyone? ... 67

3. Take care of your active listening skills ! 71
   - A. *Be interesting before being interested* 71
   - B. Think Customer! 77

4. Take care of your messages ! 81
   - A. What message are you sending? 81
   - B. FOR A JOB ADVERTISEMENT 99
   - C. Seducing the crowds : How ? 115

5. Retain your customers !...124
   A.   Satisfaction! 124

6. Take care of your project 130
   Epilogue...132

Foreword

Description and purpose of the book

When it comes to business development, we put all our strength and resources into influencing, convincing and closing deals.

There are many Personal Growth manuals and sales force management books on the subject.

Curiously, I rarely read about the medical visit.

To date, I haven't read any practical guide to professional communication between healthcare sales reps and their direct superiors.

This book is the fruit of my many readings, seminars and life experiences.

I've added real-life examples to the essential concepts.

It's the book I wish I'd received when I started my professional career in the private sector.

I hope you enjoy it.

By the way, do you like stories?

Let me tell you one first:

A certain wealthy and perceptive businessman once distributed a voucher worth €50,000 to the head of sales, €20,000 to the manager and €10,000 to the salesman, according to the abilities of each of his employees.

Before leaving on a long trip, the businessman asked everyone to develop their talents to make his assets grow in a famous banking establishment in the region where he lived.

The objective was set, the strategy defined, and he left them the means to achieve it.

A year later, he returned to take stock of everyone's performance.

Result.

The first two doubled their assets and were congratulated by management.

The last employee was severely reprimanded for his lack of initiative: he had made pitiful excuses and, after having his €10,000 taken away from him, was fired for incompetence.

The law is tough, but it's the law.

Does this story sound familiar?

You'll find it - in all proportion - in the Gospel of Matthew XXV, in the form of the parable of the Talents.

This popular wisdom reveals that we all have Skills, Acquisitions and Talents to develop.

Unfortunately, miscommunication can be very, very costly in terms of recruitment, interviews and other high-stakes negotiations.

Having and being a talent generally designates a person gifted with a valuable ability, such as art, genius, ingenuity, instinct...

I'm personally amazed to discover new vocalists and lyricists on the Paris metro, who deliver their message and emotions with ease.

Rising stars?

One thing's for sure: they believe in their talents!

Do you have any hidden talents?

A dominant talent such as :

"A talent for improvisation

"A talent for entertaining"

"A talent for selling

"Talent is having the desire".

Are you a talent, a person of value to your company?

To avoid resting on your laurels, like the passive employee in our Parable, you need to hone your talent with skills, motivation and knowledge.

Yes, everyone has talent, the trick is to find it!

The real challenge is to discover your own, the one that makes you unique!

By the way, do you have a talent for communication?

Since it seems intuitive, it's easy to <u>think you're</u> communicating.

Language is the keystone of any organized society that obeys social codes.

There are rules to effective communication that we tend to forget.

These rules are about telling stories!

Neuroscience shows that storytelling stimulates our mind, keeping our "receiving element" in suspense to find out more...or not!

So much so that the sales meeting for a salesperson can be a success... or not!

That the meeting or project can come to fruition...or not!

So, since storytelling is the most important skill, we need to "grow our assets, our talents".

In other words, to continually feed ourselves with experience, skills and knowledge.

This is what will motivate you to inspire others by choosing a direction that differs from the beaten track.

This is what will make the difference between those who give themselves the means to succeed, and those who find excuses to do nothing.

Faced with complex thinking, new processes and ever-increasing performance requirements, most managers find it difficult to find their feet...and to stand out from the crowd.

Dialogue, exchange and negotiation have never been so crucial, given the insurmountable difficulties that can arise in long-term relationships.

I'm convinced that it's possible to succeed in communicating with pleasure, method and mutual respect.

In the end, it's all about knowing yourself well enough to get the right message across at the right time, with the right tools, to make a lasting impact.

You have to learn.

So my dearest wish is to share with you the opportunity to (re)visit a few simple tools, to (re)discover how you can operate, and to turn your personal story into a strength, a unique talent by captivating your audience.

If you're a manager, you'll learn how to motivate your teams with pleasure.

No miracles, just recipes.

I don't claim to have invented these recipes, just to have put them to work for me.

How did I do it?

By making the mental effort to get out of my frame, my context, my products.

This has enabled me to better understand my customers, managers, colleagues and project partners.

It wasn't easy.

I had to fall a few times, then get up again.

Switch from solo to group mode.

If I've learned, you can too.

You too can succeed if you believe and ACT every day.

As with any art or discipline, knowledge is only as useful as its application.

I sincerely hope this manual meets your expectations.

I hope you enjoy reading it!

I wish you every success!

Frantz DALLEMAND

Introduction. Medical Sales Representatives, Regional Managers, who are they ?

"Time is the measure of business as money is of goods".

Francis Bacon, 17th century philosopher

Communication professionals who represent medical equipment and prescription and over-the-counter medicines in pharmacies, GP practices, specialists and hospitals, and are known as Pharmaceutical Representatives (**PD**), Medical Representatives (**MR**), Hospital Representatives (**HR**) or Key Account Managers (**KAM**).

I'm happy to use the term **Delegate or MR** for convenience, knowing that he's the ambassador of the laboratory he represents (whatever the structure he's approaching), and knowing that the **Manager**'s priority customers are his Delegates, whose role requires a strong presence in the field, at the heart of customer concerns.

The manager who knows how to surround himself with responsible colleagues will pass on information that will have an impact on the development prospects of the region he administers.

Generally speaking, depending on your aspirations and skills, you can progress from DP to KAM or even Manager.

This will give you an overview of an operational structure dedicated to sales.

An essential part of the pharmaceutical industry, and the interface between healthcare professionals and private companies, the **sales representative's** mission is to sell and inform, with a focus on patients.

Although it communicates indirectly to these patients, it is committed to satisfying them through the excellence of its product and accurate information.

The relay is therefore the healthcare professional, whether doctor or pharmacist, whom the Delegate must try to convince.

Medicines are not just another consumer product: they are a matter of Human or Veterinary Health!

The job of Sales Representative therefore requires a keen interest in health, in people in the medical sense, and in the pharmaceutical or hospital world, combined with a commercial sense focused on precise qualitative or quantitative objectives to be achieved.

The MR has to contact between 5 and 6 doctors a day, spend time in the waiting room, and be well-informed to encourage prescriptions.

Visits by appointment are an opportunity to discuss pathology, medico-economic news and the therapeutic strategy to be adopted for the proper use of the drug for which he is responsible.

The MR also goes to the local pharmacy to check that his product is well known by the pharmacy team, and trains them if necessary in the event of technical or pharmacovigilance difficulties.

The Hospital Delegate (DH) works in hospital structures, and according to his or her expertise has a MR role, but also a "conductor" role on cross-functional projects, deciding on medical meetings to be planned, to which doctors will call him or her.

This position requires a high level of responsibility, the ability to work as part of a team (internally with the laboratory's regional physicians or marketing departments, and externally with the healthcare teams involved in the proper use of the product), to make proposals, and to have a global vision of the medico-economic environment of the public or private structure he/she is approaching.

The Key Account Manager (**KAM**) will be responsible for working with major hospital accounts (pharmacists) to negotiate prices/volumes.

He or she may be responsible for the laboratory's molecules, or for liaising with regulatory bodies (regional health agencies, drug and device committee heads, hospital directors and pharmacists for referrals, etc.), or for facilitating relations between these different bodies, which can sometimes be quite hermetic.

The KAM is not just a salesman, he manages an account, and must build a long-term partnership.

This means being very close to the customer (the key account), who expects the KAM to be more than just a supplier of products or services.

.

Finally, the **Manager** whose job it is to lead a team, and ensure that it meets the expectations of the sales department, must steer and direct his group with finesse and tact to achieve objectives.

Its mission:

-manage a team of sales representatives, accompany them to customers to evaluate product communication.

-translate national objectives into individual regional action plans.

-monitor the implementation of these objectives and correct any discrepancies using dashboards.

-coordinate project activities in collaboration with internal and external departments.

-Participate in and prepare management meetings (annual objectives, seminars, marketing projects, debriefing of communication campaigns, etc.).

Being a manager is a very demanding job:

First and foremost, you need to be a good communicator, to know your team well, to identify the fluidity of relations between them, so that strategic information circulates between the leader and the group in the best interests of the laboratory or sales department (Business Unit), but also to carry through a project, to lead your group to success, to pass on the flame, to bring added scientific or technical value, to develop skills, to be an expert in your product, to have good analytical skills. And to be motivated!

Motivation that can be energy-consuming!

Just as all delegates have different degrees of maturity, so do all management styles!

There's a wide range of styles, from highly directive to highly participative, consensual or empowering.

In essence, the manager has to put together a "bouquet of talents" in the service of the company's financial results.

The collective born of the sum of individual talents.

Delegates are regularly monitored by precise analysis tools, thanks to dashboards on sales, sales trends, current actions, customers and backorders, etc...

At the monthly or annual appraisal interviews, the moment of truth arrives, when the manager takes stock of past performance and sets or corrects the course for the year ahead.

What all these field operatives have in common is that they all travel a lot, have great physical stamina to cope with the stress of results, are highly available, and have a strong sense of ethics and personal organization.

Analytical skills, the ability to stand back and look at the big picture, responsiveness and the ability to constantly question one's ability to communicate effectively, these are the skills you need to master!

In the long term, for those who want to make a career of it.

Assigning roles :

Delegate	Manager
Fact	Done and done
Sells	Sells
Has knowledge	Transmits knowledge
He speaks	He listens, analyzes
Perhaps self-centered	Is available
Is concerned	Secure
Has his nose to the grindstone	Assess performance

A very personal comment

Now that these professions have been described, the men and women in the field who work with healthcare professionals are occasionally caught in the crossfire between the media, their superiors and the expectations of the medical profession.

Suffering in the workplace, accused of many ills, of being poison salesmen, patient associations and, like many companies, pharmaceutical companies are not always kind!

What could be more difficult for a sales representative to hear than knowing that his or her job is misunderstood, or experiencing burnout due to misunderstandings?

Or more simply, stress at work.

Like all industries, the pharmaceutical industry can also find itself in need of care.

Not that the company is a big family to be devoted to, but on the other hand, I believe it's possible to strive for excellence in human relations on the same level as product excellence.

A number of magazines have recently started talking about "Happy Management", "Feelgood management" and benevolent talent management.

Letting talents express themselves and develop responsibly is good for business, as it stimulates a certain spontaneity and creativity in human relations.

I would like to express my wish for a new balance:

Balance between ethical consumption adapted to medical needs and overproduction of drugs with sometimes (too) iatrogenic effects.

Balancing honest sales and mercantile dealings

Balance between communication and manipulation.

A tightrope-walking exercise, if ever there was one.

The perilous exercise of the Delegate, balancing on a tightrope in the face of contradictory demands, is not an easy one:

- Working as part of a team and achieving individual goals
- Get involved and stand back
- Being creative and prescriptive
- Being an expert and a generalist

The Manager's perilous exercise is just as delicate

- Understand others better to be more convincing
- Managing personal conflicts and agendas
- Learning from your group without being intrusive

- Taking on the role of leader and giving meaning to action

Putting a little Psychology and Savoir Vivre into the Business Mechanism is therefore the lubricating oil of the Delegate and Manager profession:

It's a **VITAL** issue!

Dialogue, transparency, participation in the group, small gestures, sharing, benevolence: these are, in my opinion, the foundations of fulfilling communication.

Communication that gives meaning to the action and makes it exciting.

Confucius version:

"Love what you do and who you do it with, and you won't feel like you're working.

1. Take care of your relationships !

A. A few general points

"As an expert in my products for many years, this contract was for me!

I'm motivated by new business challenges.

As a recent business school graduate, do I have everything it takes to succeed as a sales representative?

Why doesn't my team meet my expectations?

I think I'm an efficient manager, don't you?

I have a passion for transmitting and a passion for achieving results here and now.

What am I missing?"

Have you ever had this kind of experience?

What emotions went through your mind and body?

Anger, sadness, the desire to surpass yourself despite all your skills!

Doing better?

Much better?

Perfect your professional relationships?

Without setting the bar so high, why improve the **QUALITY of** your relationships with your Partners, Customers, Suppliers, Prospects, Crew?

In such a competitive environment, how can you build **lasting** loyalty to the relationships that are so important to you and your company?

> Know this: everything you say and express has a *positive or negative influence on* your relationships with others!

Yes, you have that double-edged power!

You are therefore the architect of your own successes and failures!

Yes, the solution starts with **YOU**!

In fact, it's on you that your employer relies to develop your sector of activity, your sales, your contacts, your business.

That's why you're hired and paid!

That's why it's so urgent to take care of your communication and professional relationships, because you live from them, with them or may one day need them.

B. Why improve quality?

Imagine, for example, a world where you're alone, in charge of immense power, immense wealth, food galore, a dream property by the beach!!!

Wonderful, isn't it?

Except that this world belongs to only a few hundred families in the world whose wealth exceeds that of billions of people.

It's unfair, but it's the economic reality, and morally unequal, let's face it!

And yet, these same billionaires **depend on** others.

They depend on the resources given to them, inherited from their parents or obtained by sheer force of will.

They depend on maids to feed them, ship captains to drive them, and master hoteliers to welcome them!

However, without air, without food, such people are nothing.

NOTHING!

It's the same for all of us.

We coexist, we depend - whether we like it or not - on others, just as natural forces circulate between them: electricity, wind, air, magnetic fields, water...

Everything circulates, nothing is fixed, that's the meaning of things.

The principle is that life itself is ENERGY!

And movement, as Leonardo Da Vinci said.

Since life is all about movement and interrelation, social networking sites like Facebook, LinkedIn and Twitter have been carrying thousands of pieces of information every day for the past ten years.

Since life is movement and influence, advertising invests millions of dollars or euros to condition us through sharp, targeted neuromarketing methods.

Google, Apple and Microsoft have all understood this.

These American companies are setting the pace in the digital economy, and are now banking on the CONFIDENCE of INTERNET RELATIONSHIPS.

If you want to live in our 2.0 world, **you MUST ACCEPT** the obvious:

It's all about relationships and digital interdependence - unless, of course, you're exiled to a desert island!

Even then, you'll need an Internet connection!

Si, si for your return because you will quickly get bored without smartphone 4 G!!!!

Take stock

So why improve your interpersonal relations?

Because you simply have **no choice**!

It's as silly as that!

Just as we can't do without breathing, eating and consuming.

If you want to take advantage of circulating resources, then understand this principle well

> **It's not what COMES INTO YOUR HOME THAT'S IMPORTANT, but what STAYS OUT!**

What remains of the steps you took to build your business?

What's left of the contacts that keep you going?

"What's left of your loves?"

This principle of life is valid for all types of resources and all types of personal interrelationships.

After *these generalities*, let's get back to our business as a Delegate or Team Leader.

What is your core business?

Your core business as an operative is to effectively contact your prospects and turn them into sales!

It's about moving your team forward.

To be impactful would say marketing!

Each employee has become a real profit center, self-managing and self-responsible for strategic issues, where decisions have to be made quickly.

As you can see, from my point of view, the sales representative needs to have a balanced view of his business, and concentrate on the value-added customers within his field of action.

In the same way, the Manager must focus on the How To.

C. How can we improve quality?

Take stock now of your immediate professional environment, your partners, your customers, your managers.

What do you think, honestly?

Aren't there things that need to be reviewed?

-How can you say today that your relationships are solid?

For example, by using a simple grid listing winning behaviors that assesses where you stand with your customers or teams.

WINNING BEHAVIOR GRID

AM I AVAILABLE	Rating 1 to 5
AM I IN FEED BACK	Rating 1 to 5
AM I ON MY CUSTOMER/TEAM'S SIDE?	Rating 1 to 5
AM I GENEROUS?	Rating 1 to 5
AM I RELIABLE	Rating 1 to 5

-Am I AVAILABLE to my customer? Does he know?

> Am I in FEED BACK mode with my boss? Can I ask him from time to time what he thinks of my services?
>
> -How well do I know my customer, my partner?
>
> -Do I know his real needs?

- Will your contacts be able to defend you in case of need, assist you, support you, recommend you?

To ensure that your contact supports you, here are a few questions to ask yourself:

> -In case of difficulty, am I already on his side, before it happens?
> -Have I proved that I am reliable, that I keep my promises?
> - do I express my personality to him sincerely?

-Do you think this "damn customer" could order more, this supplier could be more generous?

So how do you get him to be more active towards you?

> -Am I already generous to him?
>
> - did I make him understand my problems?
>
> -Do I make commercial gestures towards him, in compliance with the law?
>
> -Do I find ways, not excuses, to thank this customer or supplier?

Loyalty will be the subject of chapter 5 of this manual.

Relationships fly by the seat of your pants, and you need to review where you stand periodically.

It's obvious that deteriorating commercial or intra-group relations jeopardize a company's business sector.

"Any house divided against itself will perish".

From time to time, things slide into one or more unfortunate misunderstandings with a customer, manager or supplier.

In such cases, the situation needs to be reframed or clarified as far as possible.

D. How to deal with Mr/Mrs UNHAPPY ?

You want to implement strategies to build quality relationships.

In your company, because people are pleasant.

With your customers, your partners, your colleagues.

Sometimes things don't go so well, and you find it unbearable to tolerate the little perfidies of everyday life for so long.

Since you don't deserve such "spikes", you'll have to take action at some point.

This is conflict management.

Everything can be said in the following way:

DESCRIBE	SPECIFIC FACTS
EXPRESS	EMOTIONS
SUGGEST	A SOLUTION
CONVINCE	INTERLOCUTOR

This is known as Non-Violent Communication.

Assertiveness means taking your place, no less, no more.

I respect you, respect me.

This means daring to understand the other person's situation and concerns, but also expressing emotions and feelings, and daring to say no and why.

In this way, you establish a clear and relevant relationship, assuming your role and position.

Assertiveness is the key to serenity and efficiency.

In this way, you come across as a source of proposals, as someone who adopts a positive approach, who knows how to handle complex situations, and above all, who knows how to unblock them.

EXAMPLE

-You're a women's representative and you've got a customer who's making advances, who's asking to see you outside a professional context.

-You're a young KAM and your important customer will only list your product if he receives a conference slot from you.

-Do you work with a difficult superior who plays hardball or gives his team little leeway?

What to do?

ANSWER

In all cases, remain neutral, factual, and assert your position, rights, reputation and interests.

"I feel I'm not respected by your attitude towards me, imagine your wife's reaction, I'm asking you to...".

Hiding behind a position of authority can sometimes be useful.

"Sincerely, I'd find it hard to justify your attitude/request to my management, and I'd suggest you work this way instead...".

"What I want you to do today is..."

Be careful what you say.

In fact, you may be facing :

-manipulators

-soft rags

-authoritarian psychorigids

-policies

-incompetents

-etc.

If you run away from the situation, you move the problem.

If you ATTACK, you're looking for submission.

If you MANIPULATE, you control by devious means.

So, in all cases, we recommend several winning face-to-face attitudes.

It's not about "reframing" your customer or manager in front of everyone.

- FILTER any unhealthy comments, rejecting vulgarity or lack of objectivity.
- RECADER calmly but firmly
- DEMAND a quality relationship before attacking the problem, not the person.
- REFUSE toxic or potentially toxic language
- Get respect, because your long life depends on it

Otherwise, sooner or later, you will pay the price: your lack of freedom!

Since you can't win every time, focus on the future positive aspects of a change that affects you.

There are always some.

Get away from negative people as much as possible.

They are toxic in the long term and will eat into your self-confidence.

"These are people who have a problem with every solution!

I repeat, everything you say and do influences your relationships, for better or worse, in the longer or shorter term.

Whether you want to "survive" as long as possible in a world of "nice fish", or "nasty sharks", who want to swallow you whole, all depends on the waters you enter, but above all on your ability to swim in troubled waters, when the storm of problems rises...

You'll need to be very observant and, above all, <u>very good at</u> spotting « amanites phalloïdes mushrooms » from ceps!

Here's your first job.

If you're not satisfied, move on to the next best thing.

What's more, people will never remember what you said or did, but how you made others **feel.**

What emotion you gave off as you spoke!

Joy, sadness, boredom, charisma?

Be aware of this.

So it's up to you to take the steps to become a Responsible Adult.

Don't expect others to take the first step !

ACT FIRST !

MAKE YOUR POSITIVE EMOTIONS FELT !

2. Take care of your communication !

But what does that mean anyway?

A medical waiting room in the Paris region, on a cold Wednesday afternoon in November.

A young MR is waiting for the general practitioner, who comes out of his rounds angry.

The waiting room is packed.

Pensioners, workers, impatient young children, bawling their eyes out.

One of the mothers addressed the brawler:

"Shut up, because not only are you not doing anything at school, you're disturbing everyone.

If you go on like this, you'll end up like the gentleman here"-in reference to the Medical Rep !

You can imagine the look on the salesman's face when he heard such an insult!

It's not easy to recover from this negative emotion and gratuitous insult.

We've got to get back in the saddle quickly and keep our self-control!

Your message needs to get across, and your pleasant communication needs to reflect your empathy and concern for doing the right thing.

Since you are **the Master** of your emotions, your moods, your senses, your communication, you are like a magnet!

The magnet has the power to attract or repel ferric elements, depending on the pole on which it is placed.

This is known as the Law of Attraction, which works by conditioning our minds to success using the Coué method.

My father once told me, "If you don't get good grades in class, you'll end up sleeping under a bridge.

The strength, the magnet of paternal authority.

I haven't always got good grades, and I don't sleep under bridges at all!

But I still had to fight against this negative suggestion that had permeated my mind for a while.

A. What communication is

- Just exchanging words?
- Just exchanging feelings?

But not only.

To communicate is to be a creator, a perpetual innovator

A man or woman who FIRST and foremost CREATES the CONDITIONS for a successful complex exchange.

By complex exchange, we mean an intellectual, emotional and spiritual relationship.

Before transmitting information, it is therefore necessary to ensure that it will be heard.

The constructive force of an exchange focused on a positive objective.

A negotiation, finally, in this case

Otherwise, it's just talk, blah blah blah, rumors...

Here, you don't need advice; you let yourself be carried away by the emotion, the smile, the charm of the words.

When communicating professionally, set yourself the objective of PREPARING for a successful exchange.

A success for both parties.

Nobody likes to be short-changed in a business relationship.

If you forget to prepare, you're either very good and have your mind always on alert, or...you're preparing to be...FORGOTTEN!!!!

Your interlocutor must sense your commitment and sincerity in moving forward WITH THEM, FOR THEM.

The negotiation will be successful because you <u>decide to</u> make it a 2-person affair.

For what's at stake: your request for a raise, for an exchange of goodwill, for an internal promotion, for a commercial offer.

B. The art and art of negotiation

Do you like chess?

As you know, it's a strategy game that consists in defeating your opponent by a combination of pieces, from King to Soldier, and using all your resources to penetrate your opponent's thoughts and intentions.

In negotiation, it's more or less the same concept.

Except that in negotiation, there are no deaths, no losers!

As a salesperson, you can learn the characteristics of your products - knowledge - train yourself to ask the right questions - a skill - and make a successful sale through hard work and perseverance.

In a face-to-face interview for a job or an appraisal, we need elements, game pieces, to move forward on the table of operations where interests can prove important!

Your goal:

CONVINCING IN THE INTERESTS OF BOTH PARTIES

Finding a win-win solution

Preamble: start your interview with a clear objective, with the end in mind.

Tip 1: Evaluate your room for manoeuvre

Know your opponent's strengths and weaknesses as part of your preparation.

The Internet is teeming with precise information, so try to get as much as you can about your opponent.

Once you have considered all the possible scenarios, set yourself a non-negotiable limit by preparing the *Best Spare Solution*.

Tip 2: Present your arguments

By arriving relaxed, self-confident and ready to emphasize the key points that will strike a chord in your opponent's mind, you need to DEMONSTRATE that you are the best alternative at the right time, in the interest of the person listening to you.

Tip 3: Speak little but well

Good listening skills, intellectual availability, no cell phone on - or on vibrate mode - sincerity, these are the postures of openness.

Identify his unmet needs and use strong words.

Always look for what suits the person you're talking to, and take notes to maintain a climate of trust.

Highlight the differentiating features of your product or service by integrating it into your service, development strategy or investment policy.

Tip 4: Be aware of objections

Is it too expensive? He certainly has good reasons.

Go along with them by telling them what type of customer your product is aimed at, preferably by reminding them of all the favorable arguments.

Getting a yes or at least an agreement from an open-ended question is the goal not to be missed.

The customer needs to focus on a key point that he hadn't noticed before the interview.

Make a maximum offer and go down to your starting scenario.

Tip 5: Conclude brilliantly

Summarize the whole discussion to show that you've made progress together.

Underline all points of agreement.

Remove any snags.

Add a final bonus on a deadline, that you'll do everything to fight for it etc...

Congratulate him on his choice

C. List of winning words and attitudes

Excellence

Training

Purpose

Management

Method

Synergy

Objective

Performance

Group

Players

Issues

Business conditions

Parameters

Results

Impacts

Know-how

The actions

Contribute

Communicate

Plan

Strengthen

Potentiate

Putting things into perspective

Impact

Optimize

Increase

Stimulate

Identify

After words, here are a few more winning communication actions:

My personality

My attitude

My intentions

PERSONALITY	ATTITUDE	INTENTIONS
genuine	right	direct
fatalistic	elusive	feint
manipulator	authoritarian	guilt-inducing
threatening	forward	review

- Where do I start with one of the three modules?
- What should I analyze in one of the three modules?

D. A little theory

> *What can transactional analysis do for us?*

In the 20th century, a doctor by the name of Eric Berne invented a method known as "transactional analysis", based on the idea that exchange tends towards transaction.

It highlighted the importance of :

-to know oneself fully before knowing others

-Identify the different strategies to be adapted to different types of people (in this case, our customers, partners and managers).

The psychological concepts highlighted are the postures of :

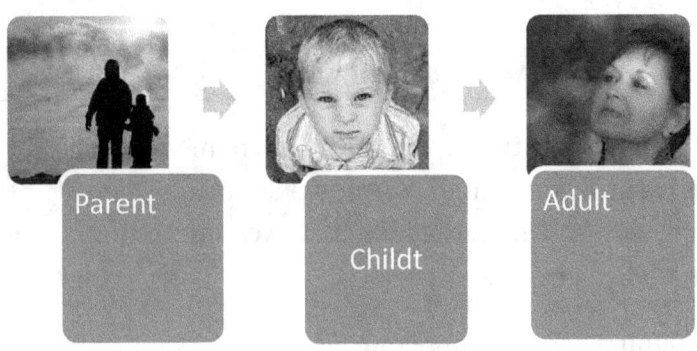

Child, Adult, Parent

E as in Child, or Emotion, or the person with this trait translates his or her existence with lilting words, or on the contrary, he or she may devalue and efface himself or herself, his or her posture is playful or withdrawn.

The Child Man is free, natural, emotional, contentious and critical.

P is for Parent, normative, which translates into value judgments, principles, advice, do this, don't do that, you should, it's stupid...

The Parent man dictates, directs, imposes.

The Parent man overprotects, congratulates, helps.

A for Adult is the man who's rather realistic and thoughtful when faced with a situation; he's calm, analytical, gives his point of view and welcomes the ideas of others.

He uses words like "It's understood, I agree, what do you want from me"?

There are interrelationships between each person

A to P

P to A

E to A

And so on.

The ideal is a mutually profitable A-to-A relationship.

Do you recognize yourself in this portrait?

How are you perceived by others?

Do you recognize your customers, teams and partners in this brief description?

So start by getting to know yourself, then classify your contacts according to their strengths and areas for improvement.

Pay more attention to our perceptions of ourselves and others.

Indeed, our idea of events is altered by our value judgments.

Everyone has their own prism of perception, which is why it's so important to observe and get to know yourself.

As the A-to-A ideal is not always de rigueur

Your job will be to subtly adapt, to match your personality to that of your partner.

To do this, you can take inspiration from this method:

Color Method

This method stems from the work of Carl JUNG, a psychiatrist in the 20th^e century, who was strongly influenced by Freud, Nietzche and others.

Jung is the pioneer of analytical psychology.

In fact, JUNG crosses many things: "Spirit" and "Action", "thought and decision", "vision to altruism, extraversion to introversion".

From this, he derived a matrix of 4 colors of psychological types, widely used today.

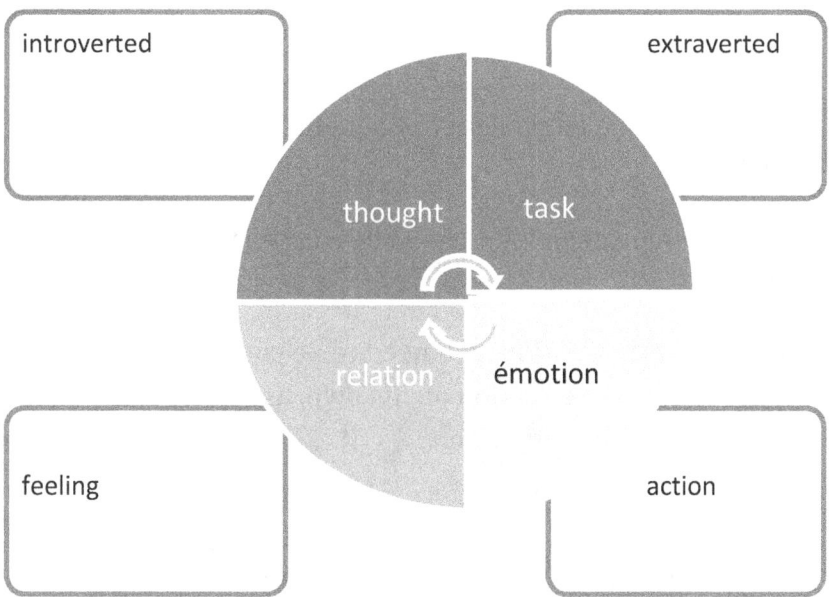

RED demands results.

He decides quickly, alone, "Time is money".

What to do with him?

A man of results, go straight to the point, because his time is short.

So avoid unnecessary chatter, as he can see far and fast.

To capture his attention, you need to be concrete and let him decide the situation on his own, as he likes to dominate complex situations.

- **Qualities:** winning, ambitious, efficient, fast, leader, responsible, courageous, expressive and rich.

- **Faults:** direct, directive, controlling, impatient, hot-tempered, insensitive, undiplomatic, pretentious, full of himself.

- **Needs:** results, performance, speed, respect and power.

EXAMPLE Bernard Tapie, french businessman

Blue demands detail

He is patient, analytical and takes the time to make decisions.

What to do with him?

When preparing your contract or file, everything needs to be checked.

As an example of pointed questions, you run the risk of being discredited by approximate answers.

Present your products and services in a methodical, rational and reassuring way.

- **Qualities:** intelligent, analytical, rational, organized, structured, orderly, responsible, respectful of regulations, reliable, punctual and persevering.

- **Faults:** very perfectionist, critical, reserved, independent, cold, distant, very weak sense of humor and very thrifty.

- **Needs:** logic, security and guarantee.

EXAMPLE Bill Gates

Yellow calls for creativity

He's enthusiastic and talkative

What to do with him?

To capture his attention, redirect the interview according to your objectives, as he has ten thousand ideas a minute and is often instinctive.

Develop an argument about his interests, because he wants to be involved.

Present your company and its products in an original, offbeat way.

Make sure you're always on hand to help with time-consuming administrative procedures.

- **Qualities:** cheerful, passionate, enthusiastic, charismatic, very social, articulate, funny, creative and likes change.

- **Flaws:** spontaneous, impulsive, disorganized, late, laggard, spendthrift, superficial, no follow-through.

- **Needs:** pleasure, prestige, play, recognition, challenge and novelty

EXAMPLE Barack Obama

Green demands attention

He's caring and reliable.

What to do with him?

To capture his attention, be sincere in your approach by showing deep emotion for his activities.

Develop an argument based on his interests, such as yellow, in addition to a sympathetic ear because he's sensitive to them.

In fact, he's a model of listening and cooperation.

Present your company and its products in a reassuring way.

Take care of the form, giving him time to think.

- **Qualities:** humane, warm-hearted, altruistic, compassionate, kind and respectful, sincere, diplomatic, good listener and environmentally aware.
- **Flaws:** traditional, hates change and risks, lacks ambition and leadership, doesn't express himself enough and lacks self-confidence.
- **Needs:** security, stability, honesty and loyalty.

-EXAMPLE Lady Diana

SAMPLE MATRIX

Professional	Intro/extra	Task/relationship	Communication	Color
M X				
M Y				

What can the Process Comm method do for us?

Inspired by Berne's work on transactional analysis, Taibi Kahler, in the 1970s, developed the following reflection:

"Why some people generate positive outcomes (reinforced motivation, stimulation to take action and achieve results, ...) while others lead to negative outcomes (demotivation, immobility, aggressiveness, depression, etc.)." source wikipedia.

This is because there are characteristic dominant personality traits.

Taibi Kalher identifies 6 dominant personality types

Worker "type" 1st arrived, last to leave

Persevering "type" very involved

Rebel "type" thinks out loud what he says

Typical luxury developer

Empathetic "type" well-being for all

Typical dreamer ...Dreamer

This method helps to identify the ideal channel for communicating under light stress as part of a joint project.

The Wiki encyclopedia identifies 4 channels.

"The affective channel: words speak of emotion, feelings, the tone of voice is calm, the attitude is smiling, relaxed and turned towards the other person.

The analytical channel: the discourse is oriented towards facts or opinions; it often contains questions, the tone is calm, without particular emotion, possibly supported by certain words (the key words of the discourse); the expression is sober, the attitude is rather rigid.

The promoter channel: lots of onomatopoeia and expressive words in speech; the tone is enthusiastic, accompanied by dynamic gestures.

The directive channel: words incite action (imperative verbs), tone and attitude are calm, with no particular emotion.

Why Process Comm?

Within a Group, this method helps to understand fundamental needs and helps the Leader to motivate or refocus his or her interlocutor.

EXAMPLES

The Dreamer

He is gifted with the power of concentration and introspection.

Silent, he can patiently put up with the silences and mistakes of others.

Her needs: Calm

The Developer

Dynamic and adaptable, he's a driving force in the group who loves challenges and aims to win at all costs.

A risk-taker on ambitious projects, he's a pioneer in search of new markets and new ideas.

Always, with panache!

Persuasive, he can wake the team up and get them going.

Its needs: challenges

E. Is your mission well understood by everyone?

As a Delegate or Manager, you will be assessed by your line manager on a project, a performance, a Key Opinion Leader, a team to be developed.

Before plunging into action, it's important to get your message across to the customer and group members.

To avoid any misunderstandings, it's important for the customer to understand the ins and outs of the mission and project.

Is the information provided well-founded, or is it just noise?

To do this, you need to be clear and simple.

EXAMPLE

You've decided to hold a sales meeting to raise a problem with an important customer.

Or maybe you've decided to invite all your customers to a medical staff meeting.

The Manager, like the Delegate, will be careful to explain what he's saying, at the risk of having his team rack their brains to find out what he thinks.

And between what the sender sends out as a message and what the receiver actually hears, many filters can intervene.

Did you say rhetoric?

According to Lionel BELLANGER, lecturer at HEC (French High Executive School) and author of "7 minutes pour convaincre" (ESF Editeur, 2006) , here are 4 points on which to excel:

1. Be clear

The first step to convincing is to explain things clearly and simply.

"What is well understood is clearly stated.

From the outset, you need to define your goal - where you're going and why.

2. Show conviction

The conviction you put into your speech adds to the power of persuasion: you put your guts into it.

It represents the commitment and personal investment you make through your own insurance.

Gestures, smiles and grandiloquence will give impact to your determination.

3. Be credible

To do this, rely on facts and evidence that add to the truth. Well-chosen examples will hit the nail on the head.

4.Be argumentative

A rhetorical exercise par excellence!

Deduction is reasoning to convince.

It consists of the following sequence:

1. - Statement of facts...

2. - "Or..."

3. - "So..."

4. - "Makes sense, doesn't it?"

Have you been set any targets?

Objectives must be **SMART**

S as in **Specific**: adapted to each individual

M as in **Measurable**: periodically assessed

A for **Accessible**: sufficiently motivating

R for **Realistic**: resources put in place

T for **Temporary**: every project has a timetable

IF YOU WANT TO COMMUNICATE SERIOUSLY, YOU HAVE TO HAVE THE MEANS TO DO SO.

Know how you work yourself

Adapt to each customer or partner

Immerse yourself in its environment

3. Take care of your active listening skills !

A. *Be interesting before being interested*

Without wood, fire goes out, that's obvious.

No fuel, no heat.

Similarly, to fuel a conversation, we need to feed and enrich what we say by taking an interest in the person we're talking to.

Well-chosen opinion questions can help.

A fatal error par excellence if you don't listen, because by not paying due attention to your employees or customers, you send out the wrong signal.

The wrong signal can lead to misinterpretation and therefore to incorrect behavior.

Identify ALL the issues and NOT just the issues.

Without, of course, attacking the people ...

Example: a customer clearly contradicts you on price, therapeutic strategy or product references.

An employee is always late for meetings or makes a point of exasperating the team.

It's up to you to take the reins of your carriage.

Another example:

"Why do you think patients are less satisfied with our campaign?

"In your opinion, what solution could be put in place to solve this or that problem?"

Of course, not everyone will be able to answer your questions, because a customer who is totally available doesn't always exist, as he's so much in demand.

Be patient, because you're creating a relationship, a project.

Over time, the person you're talking to will see you as a quality partner, and will speak up later.

FORGET YOUR SALES TECHNIQUES FOR A MOMENT: you're a Consultant!

If you don't have all the answers to your customer's or team's objections :

- Don't invent
- Don't over-promise
- Don't undervalue yourself or your company
- Don't rush

If you don't have the answers, just say you're going to do some research or ask the management.

The next time you come into contact with us, you'll be branded as a CREDIBLE and PROPOSING PERSON.

Or, on the contrary, you risk coming across as unreliable!

On the other hand, if you have an argument that hits the nail on the head, go for it!

A winning argument is an obvious one that makes the listener forget everything that's been said before, and makes him or her make the final decision to buy.

A bit of humor or a sincere compliment will add a touch of sympathy to this formal discussion.

Take careful note of all the information given to you during the interview, and record it in a file.

Over time, you'll gain valuable information about your customer

"You don't get two chances to make a good first impression!!!"

Your success depends on 3 pillars:

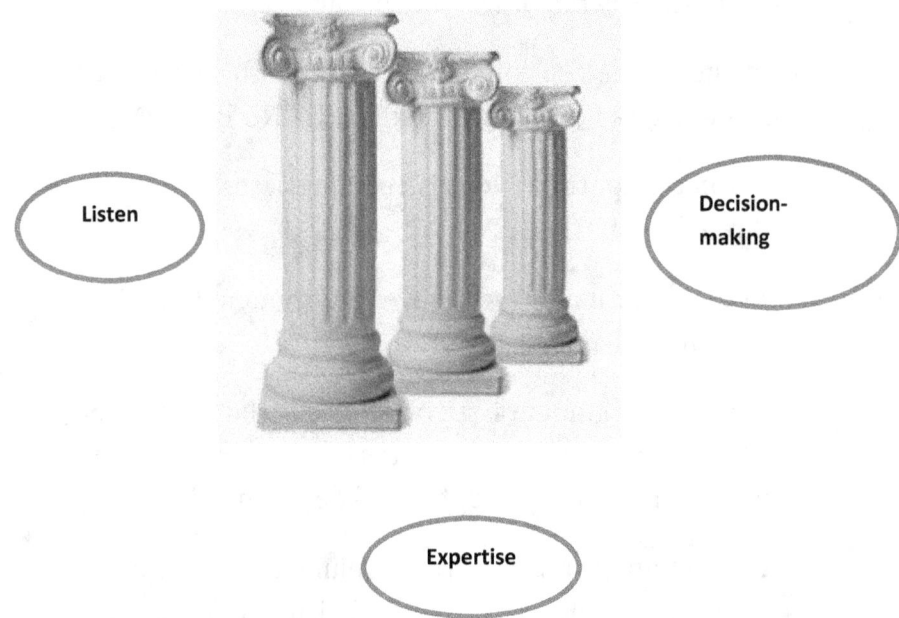

Active listening

Support your listening by nodding, rephrasing to be in phase, to discern your customer's real or hidden needs according to the **SPNCs** motivational schema.

Security

Pride

New

Comfort

Sympathy

Everyone has a deep-seated motivation.

It's up to you to find out where your customer or team is located.

If the person is interested, he or she will express this through a verbal or non-verbal intention.

Technical product expertise: You need to master the technical side of things.

The customer will ask for details (if necessary) highlighting the disadvantages of your product or service compared to the competition.

Raise the bar by gaining differential advantages over the competition on one or two specific points (delivery, reliability of follow-up teams, responsiveness of marketing department, etc.).

Decision-making: You don't force your customer's hand, because the act of buying simply validates all the steps you've taken together, by proposing several alternatives that are in line with your customer's wishes.

That's your bonus!

The purchase order can only be signed if all the steps have been followed.

With a benevolent, sincere and constructive relationship, it's no longer an act of purchase but an *investment* for your customer or supplier.

B. Think Customer!

If you have 1/4 of an hour for an interview or meeting, it's imperative that your contacts feel they're not wasting time with you.

Why?

Because they're overworked and have little time for sales.

You can be sure that your products and solutions are the best.

If you set out with your head held high, you run the risk of being objected to or quickly turned down!

To save them time, they need to feel that you fully understand their needs, that you're a reliable contact.

You need to have the end in mind:

Instead of focusing on your company, the meeting will be devoted to a specific business issue

Or an objective that mobilizes your prospect. For example, you could advertise :

EXAMPLE

Let's take the case of a sales representative who has an appointment at a hospital pharmacy.

Will he present his company, its key figures, its market positioning?

At the risk of boring your prospect, it's best to proceed as follows:

"Mr. X, as I mentioned when I made the appointment, we *help* pharmacy and hospital teams to better manage and buy...

I'd like to know what difficulties you encounter when negotiating contracts/customer transactions.

You're problem- and customer-oriented, that goes without saying.

You focus on the "Why you're here and How we do it together".

School directors, department heads and other decision-makers will immediately listen, and you'll be labeled a Life Facilitator.

During staff meetings, all you have to do is open the meeting or **presentation by helping them achieve their objectives.**

At a regional meeting, it's a good idea to make a few kind, constructive remarks about each other's work.

This helps to give an image of the values you stand for, human values.

The best thing is to know their point of view first, and then adapt accordingly.

By fully understanding their expectations, you can mobilize your teams and resources.

Conclude with a success story that highlights the results achieved by another customer/structure/collaborator thanks to your help.

Always tell your story by first focusing on what interests others.

SUMMARY

POSITIVE ATTITUDE

WARMTH AND SINCERITY

ADAPTED PERSONAL INTEREST

JOINT DECISION

4. Take care of your messages !

A. What message are you sending?

"Only those who stand out from the crowd are worthy of interest".

Gerald Tougas, Canadian writer

You're strolling through a shopping mall in a big city and enter a store that catches your eye.

You've got your heart set on that gorgeous piece of jewelry, or that suit that would fit you perfectly.

Do you like your choices to be respected when you enter the store, or do you prefer the sales assistant to jump on you as soon as you arrive?

"Can I help you?" is generally not well received by the customer.

Nobody likes to have their emotions disturbed.

Similarly, when building a joint project, do you want to get the best out of your team and win their full support?

So you need to stand out from the crowd by adding a touch of added value to make an impact in your communication at meetings, customer events and recruitment interviews.

Every message aims to touch the emotions before it touches the mind.

So you need to pay attention to every detail about yourself to maximize your impact.

YOU HAVE 2 MINUTES TO CONVINCE

Your clothes, your hairstyle, your make-up, your jewelry, your briefcase, the way you store your documents, your car all betray a state of mind.

Orderly or chaotic.

Clean or dirty.

Serious or casual.

Why 2 minutes?

Because the ability to maintain focus on you is short!

A positive attitude of openness is

Happy

Warm

Relaxed

Confident in herself

These few qualities will have a powerful effect.

The opposite is also true (anxiety, rigidity, pessimism, vanity, etc.).

THE NON VERBAL

In less than 30 seconds, the team, customer or recruiter will scan you and compare your verbal message (30% of your communication) with your posture, the way you radiate (60% of your communication).

Your contact will pay particular attention to :

Your handshake, firm or soft

Your smile and sincere sense of humor - it'll show in your eyes - with moderate outbursts, or you'll be spotted.

Your physical posture, your hairstyle, your facial expressions reveal your personality.

Your voice is rhythmic, your legs are firmly planted on the ground, your eyes are directed at the person (otherwise you're talking into a void), your hands are open and your arms are wide.

It's all these details that will make you look good!

YOUR LOOK

Do you feel like you're not succeeding at interviews?

Have you thought about the way you look?

"Tell me how you dress and I'll tell you who you are".

Since you're sending out an implicit message, the codes of success require you to work on your physical appearance and dress.

Cleanliness, a trimmed beard, well-groomed hair and discreet perfume will give a good impression of you.

Even when you've got all those diplomas, your looks can do you a disservice if you're not careful.

The dress-code is therefore to dress appropriately for your professional environment.

Sober, or chic with common sense.

What's important is that you're elegant, well-dressed and comfortable expressing yourself.

A suit that makes you look your best.

Fluorescent tights, chewing gum, an unshaven face or a mismatched skirt are all inappropriate and suggest a lack of taste, or a casual attitude, which you'll express to customers and in meetings.

A touch of originality is allowed, to stand out from the crowd.

It can be a beautiful object (ring, watch, cufflinks, scarf, etc.).

FOR BUSINESS MEALS

At a business lunch, you don't talk about your life "in detail", or that of your competitors, unless the person you're talking to speaks directly on the subject.

In this case, always remain factual without trying to denigrate.

Be punctual and watch out for alcohol.

Generally speaking, we get to the heart of the matter after a few words about our guest's health, the weather or local gastronomy.

YOUR SLOGAN

During maintenance, it is a good idea to :

Say what you're going to say

Saying what you have to say

Saying what we had to say

To be differentiating, your message must contain a USP :

YOUR UNIQUE SELLING PROPOSITION

According to the "conseilmarketing.com" website, you must answer these types of questions:

Who are you?

What are you doing?

How would you describe your business from the customer's point of view?

What benefits do you bring?

What's your added value?

Who are your competitors?

What makes you different?

What is your customers' number 1 problem?

What makes you unique?

What do your customers like best about your products?

What feedback do they give you?

How do your managers perceive you?

In any case, remain an open-minded person.

YOUR E-REPUTATION

It's impossible to ignore the use of digital products today.

Facebook: 1.65 billion monthly users

YouTube: 1 billion users per month

LinkedIn: 400 million users per month.

These 3 fast-growing sites illustrate the shift that modern society is currently undergoing.

You need to fit in, because any recruiter will use a search engine to see who you are, by cross-referencing information about you.

Social networks are a great opportunity to put you in touch with managers more experienced than you are, mentors who can help you develop your career... as long as you master the codes.

First, you must be prepared to expose yourself, honestly and factually.

Being ready to say more about yourself, your background, your goals, your projects, will inform your community.

A nice photo of yourself, with your slogan, a few recommendations from your partners or superiors and a few key words in your presentation will be enough to get you noticed by headhunters.

Secondly, keep your network alive.

Use instant messaging to post a comment or analysis on a specific issue in your field of activity.

"Make your painting an Opening to the world"
Leonardo Da Vinci.

WHAT'S YOUR ADDED VALUE?

There's no such thing as an ideal manager or collaborator.

Everyone's role is to be the bearer of meaning, of a project to achieve results.

-Types of managers

Manager typology is generally defined by 4 styles.

Leaders love power, leading and governing.

His words are strong, powerful and influential.

The Organizer likes methods, analytical

He speaks in rules, with laws, with plans.

The Cooperator loves and cares for the group

He talks about collective contribution

The Competitor likes results.

He handles personal conflicts well and turns them into strengths.

Nowadays, benevolence is the quality that produces the most results, because it focuses on the basic need for recognition for one's contribution.

Here are a few ideas for taking on the role of benevolent manager:

- He is honest in his behaviour

    -He is grateful for the work done, listens and thanks

    -He's friendly, understanding and supportive.

    -He is a driving force, sets the course

    -He doesn't take himself too seriously, and uses humor from time to time.

As managers are not always listened to by their colleagues, caught up and absorbed by the constraints of "Do more with less", "Go faster, higher, stronger", they are left with ethics, respect for others, the essence of motivation: exemplarity through benevolence.

-How can you make your staff more dynamic?

By being a benchmark in line with the identity of the company you represent.

Trust, honesty and admitting mistakes are essential.

Start by saying thank you, goodbye, get people involved, set an example, get rid of toxic substances, encourage autonomy, be flexible, ask for a "360°" (an anonymous evaluation of your own image as a manager), develop skills, etc.

As soon as the needs of each member of the group are satisfied, the manager will mobilize each member, respecting his or her own way of doing things and recognizing each person's place in the dynamic.

Any well-informed manager will prefer the stakes of a company (pleasant work, hierarchy that listens, desire to grow in a competitive environment, meaning given, clear objectives) to the primary needs of each individual (salary, benefits, status, small comforts, etc.).

Remember that it's up to each individual to motivate him or herself, and not to depend on any one entity.

It's up to each individual to find his or her motivation and share it with the group, because a motivated individual is communicative and good for his or her interests.

The leader must value contributors, those who put the group's interests before their own image, those who place responsibility before individual performance.

In this way, the group will have a soul, will be alive.

With a balance assured by the chef, between power steering and interpersonal skills.

- *Employees, define your value!*

What's important to you?

What's important to your company?

Here are a few ideas

Your personal values (success, teamwork, moral, material, human, psychological)

Your professional values (degree of autonomy, degree of organization, degree of team spirit, sales development skills)

How can you make your values bear fruit?

By being aware of your talents, your personality, your successes, your methods, your passion, your abilities.

By putting them to work on a common project.

Why?

Because it's the "How you do it" that the Manager will come looking for...

DO YOU HAVE LEADERSHIP SKILLS?

Do you know what Alexander the Great, Napoleon, General de Gaulle and Steve Jobs have in **common**?

A personality off the beaten track.

Talents of storyteller, tribune and genius who wanted to leave their *mark in the service of a cause.*

What these extraordinary talents have in common is an optimistic outlook, a broad horizon and an *ambition to serve others*.

They have blazed an uncharted trail, and their influence has left its mark on people's minds.

Generosity and benevolence for certain leaders.

Authority, megalomania for others.

Their strong point: bringing people together under their banner, federating the group.

Do you want to have leadership and influence over others?

With passion?

You don't have to be a great CEO; anyone can take on this role.

A few simple keys

Understand yourself and ask your friends and professional contacts for an assessment, advice and feedback.

Acquire knowledge, skills, a new language, specialties outside your field of vision.

Helping others by teaching, conducting interviews or helping people in difficulty.

Be benevolent in passing on ideas, concepts and learned solutions with patience.

Broaden your vision by asking top performers to share their best habits, practices, tips and success stories.

Understand others, be authentic, don't act like an egotist, have an image of a future, a radiant path.

That's leadership.

So you need to draw inspiration from all the leaders who have shaped your own existence to bring your mission, your projects and your message to life.

Have you identified one now that speaks to you?

If you have the ability to tell your story, your Personal Legend, well, that will naturally attract your group to you, so you'll be able to influence them towards your goals.

By being enthusiastic, spending time with your customers and colleagues, sharing and contributing your expertise, your difference, your Personal Touch.

With passion and consistency in what you say and do, of course.

That's what will set you apart from your competitors.

Cultivate this strength and you'll shine in your market, for your customers and your partners.

NOT TO BE DONE : NOT BEING YOURSELF

Do you want to be a leader, the one who shows the way?

Or a mere executor?

Bravo, great goal to set yourself.

A leader is not a superhero!

He's always learning, helping others, understanding their weaknesses, but giving generously of his time and resources.

Take the example of great political and religious leaders.

They serve their cause, their nation, their ideal.

They transcend and are appreciated for what they are!

If you want to be like them, take the path of authenticity and kindness!

Smooth talkers, hucksters and other bullshitters are soup sellers, specialists in the "fog pump"!!!!

Please don't be like them.

Be true, be sincere, be a help in time...

And then, yes, you'll score points.

And for a long time.

Not easy to put all these points into action on a daily basis, I admit!

I've made a few errors of judgement myself.

Some validated by my bosses!

It happens, because if you don't do anything, you'll never take the risk of making a mistake!

I'm like you, dear readers: I train, I fall, I get back up and, above all, **I LEARN**.

Conclusion

Communication is an everyday business, not a barroom chat.

You have to work day in, day out.

This is the school of everyday life, which I share with you through my experiences.

In fact, I've come to realize that the Medical Visit is a subtle balance that's very difficult to maintain, but accessible.

A difficult long-term exercise.

My final quote:

"Provided we learn from our past mistakes, the path surrounded by pebbles is always accessible!

You just have to change your shoes to go far!

B. FOR A JOB ADVERTISEMENT

Sample application:

"Based on a defined area, you prospect, sell and build customer loyalty.

You will establish a genuine partnership with them to develop your sales in line with the Company's sales policy.

In collaboration with brand coordinators, you organize operations.

With advanced commercial training, you have at least 5 years' experience as a pharmaceutical representative in the sector.

You have excellent interpersonal skills, are customer-oriented, self-reliant and organizationally rigorous.

We're looking for advisors with a genuine commercial temperament, a flair for negotiation, a strong sense of ethics, and the ability to listen and analyze in order to provide valuable advice and solutions to demanding customers.

- Efficient and dynamic, your excellent sales and results-oriented skills will enable you to meet and even exceed your targets.

As a true developer, you canvass to develop your customer portfolio.

What are the key points of this announcement?

Strong AND well-chosen words.

Partnership, collaboration, excellence, autonomy, rigor.

By mirror effect, you need to be able to demonstrate that you're 80% of the profile we're looking for.

What should attract the recruiter is your personality, which emerges from your cover letter.

Cover letter using the same winning terms.

Highlight it with your

-<u>Genuine motivation</u>: why did you choose this company, and how do you plan to get involved personally or as part of a team?

Your rich and varied personal qualities will be magnetic if you bring them to light.

-<u>Style and spelling</u>: mistakes in French or syntax generally go unnoticed.

Banish the "Hello" or "Dear Sir" style of e-mail without knowing the contact's name.

-<u>A sense of the essential</u>: the aim of a cover letter is to make the recruiter want to know more about you, your story, your career path. How will you help them achieve their goals?

Don't say everything in a letter, save some for the oral presentation.

The interview will focus on your personality, your innate and acquired skills, and your deep-rooted motivations.

In doubt? Have the body of the message reread to get straight to the point, which is to land a date!

There are no questions to avoid in an interview, but some questions are awkward or badly formulated.

Questions that are too broad or simplistic, such as sales figures or the company's business lines, can be a disservice to the candidate, who is expected to have researched the company before coming for an interview.

Asking real, more specific questions about the company's strategy, its market position, its strengths and weaknesses, its international development strategy, etc. are questions that will not only provide useful answers for you, but will also demonstrate to the recruiter your involvement and interest in the position, as well as in the company as a whole.

These are the questions most often asked during job interviews for Medical and Pharma Reps positions.

1- Introduce yourself and tell me about your background

Question asked to observe the candidate's elocution and check whether there is any discrepancy between what he says and what he has mentioned on his CV.

Be concise, and focus on the major missions relevant to the job in question.

Ex: 3 years with X where I learned management, how to draw up an action plan, customer management...

Illustrate with a specific example and dates of the results obtained.

Don't tell your life story!

Otherwise, the recruiter will have a hard time sorting things out!

2-What do you think a medical check-up is?

_ sell the drug and increase the company's sales in an ethical and strategic way, in strict compliance with legislation.

Your passion for sales or training will add a little emotion to the interview!

3-Why do you want to do this job?

No philosophy, just salary and living conditions!

If you have sales experience, highlight it with examples of previous positions.

If you have a more scientific profile, show your talents for adaptation, ready to learn a relational profession.

4- Are you prepared to change your place of residence to suit the requirements of the job?

-Be sincere and show your commitment, according to your personal constraints.

5- What is your personal contribution to our company?

_ question asked to see how the candidate will sell his or her qualities.

Talk about your values, skills and experience.

Show how you see your job, how you know how to work in a team!

6- How do you see yourself in 5 years or what are your plans?

Trick question!

_ First of all, I want to keep my job, get to know my sector, my doctor's portfolio, my colleagues...then, depending on the development opportunities the company offers me, the ideal is to become a senior sales representative or, if possible, a senior sales representative.

This is the time to ask questions about the company's medium-term development, and to position yourself as a credible reference.

7-If you find a more interesting position, will you leave the company?

"Interesting how"?

let the person you're talking to speak, this will give you an idea of his or her priorities, and you'll respond accordingly.

Why change for the salary alone, stability and well-being in the company is important, I want to **evolve** to reach higher degrees, the bottom line I will not change immediately, maybe after 5 years ask me again.

8- Why you and not another candidate?

Never denigrate candidates you don't know, even if you think you're more competent and experienced.

9- What are your personal achievements?

Don't leave anything out, even if it's extra-professional. Ideally, you should talk about it during your personal presentation.

Of course, it has to be directly related to the position you're applying for.

10- What are your faults?

_ Or areas for improvement, never talk about personal weaknesses, always talk about areas to improve according to the requirements of the job, for example: poor English, lack of organization, problems communicating in public, managing priorities, decision-making...etc.

It reflects self-knowledge and the desire for personal development.

Another question, "in burst mode":

- What is your family situation?
- Do you have children? What kind of childcare do you need?
- When are you available?
- If I ask you to start on Monday at 6 a.m., can I count on you?
- At what salary are you prepared to come to work?
- Why did you leave your last job?
- Why do you want to work for us?
- How long have you been looking for work?
- Why should I hire you?
- What do you like about working as a medical representative?
- In a few words, what is MR's position?
- Are you mobile?
- What geographical area are you willing to travel to work in?
- Are you ready for repetitive tasks?
- You're very experienced, you might get bored with us ...,
- You don't have much experience, so what are your strengths?
- Do you prefer to work alone or in a team? Why?
- If a customer gets impatient and angry, how do you react?

- What difficulties have you encountered in your previous positions?
- What do you expect from your direct manager?
- When someone criticizes your work, how do you react?
- Are you versatile?
- Do you have any health problems?

A few questions for the recruiter:

- What are the company's development plans?
- What is its growth in sales and headcount?
- What is the next step in the recruitment process, and how soon will he get back to you?

FIND THE RIGHT CONTACTS

As with any project, you have to learn the detective business.

Mentors, experts, teachers and network leaders will help you make progress towards your goal.

Don't forget "life facilitators" like medical secretaries, care nurses and administrative managers.

These people can provide you with valuable information or introduce you to their network.

In fact, they know what's going on in the system you're entering.

Make them your allies and thank them for their kindness.

BE OBSERVANT

Do you remember Sherlock HOLMES, the famous detective?

He always had his magnifying glass with him to examine the smallest details!

Get inspired!

For example, with customers.

At least at first, you meet strangers as you enter the dispensary or practice.

A smile and a friendly greeting will help create the non-verbal conditions for a favourable exchange.

But more is needed.

If you're desperate to discuss a subject on your mind, without taking into account what's on your customer's mind, how will he or she react?

Quickly discern his EMOTIONS (joy, sadness, panic, good mood) and the general AMBIANCE that lends itself to good communication (people, patients, regular phone calls...).

BE ATTENTIVE TO QUESTIONS/OBJECTIONS

A question is an open invitation!

Thanks for the objection, I'm moving on!

In fact, questions and objections are unique opportunities to probe what's on your customer's mind.

GOLDEN RULE

Emotional neutrality

Understand the objection: don't take it personally.

Discern your intentions: to get you stuck or to move forward with you by solving a serious problem?

Rephrase to make sure you've understood the meaning of the terms, to help you choose the right words and media to move the debate forward.

Answer briefly without hesitation.

For example, when interviewing for a job

. "Can you tell me how your superiors see you? "

A tough question: where to start?

The recruiter wants to see how adaptable you are, how you can turn the tables and put yourself in their shoes.

No question is insignificant.

Your answer must use an example that allows you to extract elements from your personal environment to match them with the position to be filled, which requires analysis and perspective.

What the recruiter wants is to gauge your distance from your surroundings, your breadth and height of vision.

"Tell me your personal story?"

Faced with an open-ended question, you need to seize the opportunity to highlight your personality, your professional history, or your assets that are not detected in your CV.

Come to the interview with your strengths, and present yourself with a clear and positive idea of your strengths.

Don't just assert that you're a gifted organizer, prepare concrete examples of situations or projects you've managed that convincingly demonstrate this organizational ability, and that you know how to put it into practice in the field.

If you have a complaint, see "How to talk to Mr Disgruntled".

Telephone and email meeting skills

Elegance in clothing

Warm relationships

Are you cultured?

FOR EXCELLENT PRESENTATIONS, TAKE YOUR INSPIRATION FROM THE BEST!

Are you curious enough to type "Steve Jobs" into a search engine?

124 million results (datas from 2016)

Now type "Medical rep"!

131,000 results!

1,000 times less!

The figure speaks for itself: Steve Jobs, with his charisma, his sense of major innovation and a new business model, revolutionized the world of computing!

It "scrapped" older computer models, inspired people to see the world differently, and was a serious competitor to Microsoft and IBM.

And remember, this is the USA, land of the dollar god on the altar of business-king!

Those who want to shake up the leaders have their work cut out for them.

I'm convinced that we all have a lot to learn from this man, who despite his execrable character (an understatement) gave life and soul to an extraordinary company, the Apple company ;)

Abandoned as a child, Steve Jobs became a man totally devoted to the cause of his Revolution, business and money.

Greedy, egotistical, quick-tempered, he turned his deep wounds into strength.

Able to track down the slightest marketing errors, to perversely wound others in order to humiliate them, Steve Jobs was not known for his modesty!

His personality is the subject of further debate...

In this post, therefore, I'm only going to focus on what I feel is necessary for our profession.

Here it is:

As you know, it's important for us to put ourselves forward, with a clear understanding of the situation.

What's remarkable for us Delegates, who put ourselves on stage on a daily basis, is to *market and dramatize our skills* and desires, and to convey a quality message.

How did Apple's founder electrify the crowds?

How can we draw inspiration from this formidable ability to hold the attention of our doctors?

C. Seducing the crowds : How ?

One of S Jobs' strengths in his presentations was to tell a captivating story!

Get people interested by raising an issue.

"There Is Something in the air" to open up the feeling of power, to prepare minds for what's about to be presented.

"Today, Apple is going to reinvent the Phone" sets the tone for the subject.

It's hard-hitting, and makes you want to know more.

All too often, delegates start off with a clear head, "I'm going to talk to you about X or Y", while healthcare professionals are still preoccupied with their day-to-day worries.

The theme has to be clear, the objective set, so that the audience understands where the delegate is taking them.

You can also start with :

"3 things I'd like to see with you!"

The rule of 3 key messages presented with passion makes you want to come along.

In his presentations, each section was carefully weighed and effectively introduced the other, with impeccable dialectic.

Coordinating conjunctions linked the discourse.

Every word is **strong,** like "Extraordinary, formidable, incredible".

Repeated over and over again, the ad permeated the crowd.

A very important point that VMs too often forget!

Selling a story, an experience, not a product, is the best strategy.

Delegates don't sell products, they sell concepts, dreams and solutions for patients.

How and why the product will enrich patients' lives or simplify those of medical teams.

The Delegate is a Teacher and brings a different perspective.

Yes, the delegate teaches differently!

He has a talent for transforming images!

Make statistics, figures, tables, something understandable, something that makes sense.

Why?

Every human memory has 3 components: visual, auditory and sensory.

The delegate must carefully highlight the channel preferred by his audience.

Saying that the product reduces mortality by 25% is just a bunch of numbers.

Chinese ☐ Too Abstract !

A shopping list board, filled to the brim, devalues the story.

It's ILLISIBLE, especially when it's a Power Point bulleted list!

On the other hand, making comparisons with everyday life, and illustrating what you're saying, adds depth and life to your presentation, and makes it simpler than using technical jargon.

For example, such and such a product you sell has such and such a virtue.

Saying that it makes life easier for patients and doctors in terms of compliance or some other concrete aspect is better.

"1 in 4 patients alive after one year of treatment" sounds better.

"The computer is the bicycle of thought.

It's up to you to find what best suits your argument.

"The supreme art is to keep it simple" said Leonardo da Vinci.

So keep it simple.

Sport, technology, music, art... there's no shortage of subjects.

Excellence for every product.

The story is the only thing that counts in our storytelling!

I think we can draw heavily on this experience to score favorably against the competition.

Of course, medicine is not a product like any other, and as such, scientific rigor is essential when drawing analogies.

In fact, the medical check-up charter prohibits any unproven, derogatory comparisons.

Doctors are no fools, and know very well the

difference between Promotion and Information.

Legislation on advertising regulates medical promotion, so there's no room for abuse of Transparency Commission Notices or Legal Notices.

What else to remember in meetings ?

A perfect SCENIC PICTURE

Showing off is essential.

Stage presence, body language that backs up his words.

A recognizable outfit: black sweater, jeans, sneakers.

Alone on stage, Steve Jobs knows how to stack the odds in his favor.

He's one with the audience, strolling along with ease.

A picture is worth a thousand words.

A logo or brand representative must be used and used again.

Look at the Apple.

You don't need to ask a 6-year-old what that means.

Spontaneously, he associates the logo with the company **and, above all, with the products that go with it.**

Iphone, Ipad, Ipod, McBook

He even used a clear envelope to brilliantly demonstrate McBook's size!!!

It's a real selling point that knocks out the competition.

No need for complex figures.

The message got through because "what you see sells.

A streamlined presentation, but rehearsed hundreds of times because he knew his subject inside out.

In hospital corridors, doctors are quick to spot us or...avoid us.

No time, no desire, too many patients, too many constraints.

If you're not seen as **Valuable and Worthwhile**, there's no point in believing.

The doctor won't stop.

It will stick an image to what you are, and especially not the one you think !

See my post on "Delegates and Added Value."

And how do you distinguish yourself in the pharmacies or establishments you frequent?

HOW DO YOU TALK?

Again, language is only 10% of what will be retained by the audience.

So: short, simple sentences, no technical jargon, sober but synthetic when necessary, and analytical when appropriate, will SUPPORT what you're saying.

By conveying your emotions and feelings, you will be perceived as credible and AUTHENTIC.

Prepare, read and reread your texts!

This will allow you to leave the text relaxed!

A touch of humor adds to the fun!

Too many VMs are still a little stressed about public speaking!

That's charisma for you!

So, TO CONVINCE, LET'S GO!

3 questions

- What are you wearing?
- What kind of presence do you have?
- What dialectic do you use?

3 Tips

--To be interesting

--Solving a problem

--Propose concrete benefits

--Get physically involved

In my opinion, all these points are what should characterize a high value-added Medical Sales Representative.

"Have the courage to follow your intuition and your heart.

Think differently.

Fail again, fail better.

Only those crazy enough to change the world can do it!

5. Retain your customers !

A. Satisfaction!

Now we come to the last part of our reflection.

It's been proven that loyal customers are the most profitable, and that being virtuous and honest always pays off.

In a tough environment, the cost of acquiring a customer eats up time and resources.

Maintaining a relationship is therefore less onerous than prospecting, and the same applies to your employees, where commitment depends on the recognition you give their work.

How many times have we been disappointed by the casual attitude of some people who, once the deal is done, pay us little or no attention.

Those who make a long-term commitment to providing a high-quality, personalized, attentive service to their customers or colleagues will transform their contacts into successful long-term relationships.

Customer satisfaction is therefore a vital issue for any company operating in a competitive sector.

Because simply satisfying a customer is not enough to build loyalty, and also because they have a choice, the aim is to go further with those who have the greatest development potential (purchase, prescription, recommendation).

This means offering a higher quality, higher value-added service, rather than "sprinkling" a little with everyone else.

Prioritizing is therefore essential.

So how do we go further?

Only a quality of service based on product excellence, professional competence, irreproachable attitude and mutual respect in the service of patients will make the difference.

Everyone deserves to be recognized for what they are, at their true value.

How do you look after your customers?

This is also the case when a Manager asks his troops to see higher, further, stronger.

The quality of service required will be built on the excellence of the customer's behavior.

Referring to the work of C JUNG, or that of Berne, we need to adapt in an adult way by personalizing the relationship, responding in a specific way to the needs of our customers or partners, and especially our high potentials.

By being considerate...

For a meeting :

-A Meeting, a Seminar:

- Never after 6 p.m. on a Friday before the vacations...
- An agenda is drawn up with a list of participants.
- A clear report is sent to everyone with time-defined missions.

-A professional relationship

When organizing a high-potential customer meeting :

-Choose the right topic with him, an expert topic that will appeal to the majority of guests.

Choose the right location and local cuisine, while respecting the tastes of potential high-flyers.

-Prepare the scenarios to be discussed down to the last detail

-During the meeting, pay attention to everything that is said or done.

-At the end of the meeting, collect their comments and points for improvement.

-Plan to evaluate his satisfaction or comments within a fortnight

-Put forward your arguments or requests for more "intense" work

For an assessment :

Have you developed a sought-after skill, exceeded your sales targets or taken on additional responsibilities?

This puts you in a strong position to ask.

That's right,

- The rules of the game are well established
- Your manager or colleague is available to listen to your comments

- Your manager doesn't approach salary increases as a "dilettante".
- He sets the course and discusses the details with you.

SUMMARY OF KEY PRINCIPLES

GETTING TO KNOW YOUR CUSTOMERS

BE CREATIVE

BE RESPECTFUL OF CHOICES AND A FORCE FOR PROPOSALS

BEING A LIFE FACILITATOR

6. Take care of your project

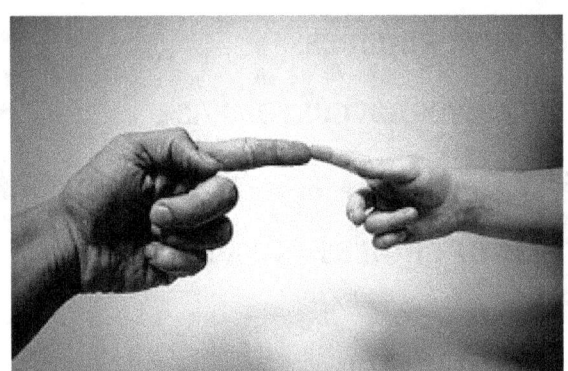

Like any good project manager, think partner.

Effective decision-makers are always interested in ideas, insights and information that help them solve their problems and achieve their goals.

To form a high-performance workgroup, the project manager will appoint a Leader, a Pilot, a Coordinator, a Thinker and a Communicator.

The project manager's missions

- project coordination, linking different times and different partners.

- formation of the team and determination of each person's duties.

- activation of partnerships (inventory of available and missing skills within the institution)

- task scheduling

- search for financing

- formalization and drafting of work and decisions.

- human resources management

Epilogue

"If you have dreams, fight to protect them, because incapable people will do anything to discourage you from achieving them."

Have you seen the film :

The Search for Happiness, starring Will Smith ?

He plays a salesman desperately trying to make a living selling scanners while looking after his four-year-old son.

With only $21 in his account, one day he comes across a trader and asks two simple questions:

What do you do and how do you do it?

This is his chance. His only chance to get out of this unbearable situation he's putting his son through. Sometimes, all it takes is a few minutes to drastically change your life.

In the film, Will Smith uses them to impress his audience.

In this way, he protects his own life and that of his son.

Steering your professional life has never been so hard.

managing our own talents and those entrusted to us is a daunting task.

To be a talent:

Keeping our talents:

Remaining oneself, as a free, adaptable individual, aware of one's skills, are the keys to success.

Staying active throughout your career is a challenge.

The road is long, constantly changing, and fraught with pitfalls.

To avoid waking up "has-been", it's best to be proactive

I've learned a lot in my 20 years of experience as a Pharmaceutical Representative, City/Hospital Medical Representative and Coach.

Since the abundance of books, seminars and techniques is immense, I took - and still take - full advantage of these tools with passion and great curiosity, accumulating numerous notes.

I've had the pleasure of working with the medical profession, training pharmaceutical and hospital staff and developing accounts for major international groups.

I've had the privilege of learning from both general practitioners in the field and university hospital specialists.

Men and women equally devoted to their passion.

Men and women in white coats at all levels, who don't count their time despite the complaints and complaints of patients, laboratories or administration.

I have enormous respect and friendship for those whose paths I crossed in the corridors of the hospitals I visited.

A real privilege!

Privileged access to scientific knowledge, to publications, to works that are the subject of symposia in places where access to the general public is very restricted.

Access restricted because it's expensive.

Places are scarce and represent a real advertising investment for pharmaceutical companies.

At first, I was impressed by the aura of the medical professors.

Then I understood better how to add value, which started by staying in my place.

By not disguising myself, by not changing my values.

Looking back over my career, I've had some great professional successes.

In collaboration with the marketing departments, I launched effective drugs on the regional market, in the treatment of seasonal flu or the management of patients suffering from hepatitis C.

Not only did I have the means to carry out my projects, but also the confidence of my hierarchy, so I was able to diversify my contacts, with other partners in my speciality and various suppliers recognized in their field.

Trade shows and forums have helped create valuable, high value-added relationships.

I've also experienced stinging failures, including one in the obesity market and in the management of chemo-induced anemia, very often due to a lack of preparation, training and projects.

Maybe I didn't believe in it enough.

It's always in difficulty that we learn best, because it generates frustration.

What solutions can we find when we can't move forward?

How do you keep the flame burning?

What are the best methods for inspiring and motivating my contacts to achieve my goals?

How to use their talents, basically.

Intuitive at first, I came to understand that "it's what we think we already know that prevents us from learning" Pr Bernard.

I didn't understand the complexity of the environment and I lacked assertiveness.

Do you have enough self-confidence to believe that you are more gifted than others?

That you, Healthcare Salespeople, have a talent?

Think about it...

Ponder, too, this last quote from Sir Winston Churchill, British statesman and pragmatic poet in his day:

Success is not final, failure is not fatal: it's the courage to continue that counts.

That's what I really wish for all of you!

Frantz Dallemand

Thanks to :

« Seven habits effective people », Stephen Covey

"Great Leaders grow: Becoming a Leader for life "

Mark Miller, Ken Blanchard

www.ingramcontent.com/pod-product-compliance
Lightning Source LLC
Chambersburg PA
CBHW082334220526
45470CB00008B/2507